CROMWELL DIXON'S Sky-Cycle

JOHN ABBOTT NEZ

G. P. PUTNAM'S SONS

For my dad, George Nez,
a pilot from the good old propeller days . . .

G. P. PUTNAM'S SONS
A division of Penguin Young Readers Group.
Published by The Penguin Group.
Penguin Group (USA) Inc., 375 Hudson Street, New York, NY 10014, U.S.A.
Penguin Group (Canada), 90 Eglinton Avenue East, Suite 700, Toronto, Ontario M4P 2Y3, Canada (a division of Pearson Penguin Canada Inc.).
Penguin Books Ltd, 80 Strand, London WC2R 0RL, England.
Penguin Ireland, 25 St. Stephen's Green, Dublin 2, Ireland (a division of Penguin Books Ltd.).
Penguin Group (Australia), 250 Camberwell Road, Camberwell, Victoria 3124, Australia (a division of Pearson Australia Group Pty Ltd).
Penguin Books India Pvt Ltd, 11 Community Centre, Panchsheel Park, New Delhi - 110 017, India.
Penguin Group (NZ), 67 Apollo Drive, Rosedale, North Shore 0632, New Zealand (a division of Pearson New Zealand Ltd).
Penguin Books (South Africa) (Pty) Ltd, 24 Sturdee Avenue, Rosebank, Johannesburg 2196, South Africa.
Penguin Books Ltd, Registered Offices: 80 Strand, London WC2R 0RL, England.

Library of Congress Cataloging-in-Publication Data
Nez, John A.
Cromwell Dixon's Sky-Cycle / John Abbott Nez.   p. cm.
Summary: In 1907 Columbus, Ohio, fourteen-year-old Cromwell Dixon, aided by his mother, begins building the flying bicycle he has invented to enter
in the St. Louis Air Ship Carnival. Includes facts about Dixon's life as an aviation pioneer. Includes bibliographical references.
1. Dixon, Cromwell, 1892–1911—Juvenile fiction. [1. Dixon, Cromwell, 1892–1911—Fiction. 2. Air pilots—Fiction. 3. Flying machines—Fiction.
4. Inventors—Fiction. 5. Flight—Fiction. 6. Aeronautics—History—Fiction.] I. Title.   PZ7.N4882Cro 2009   [E]—dc22   2008026140

ISBN 978-0-399-25041-5
10 9 8 7 6 5 4 3 2 1

Columbus, Ohio, 1907

Cromwell Dixon was a born inventor.

As sure as electricity makes sparks, you could find him hard at work on some new invention in the old barn behind his house.

"Cromwell has always been of a mechanical nature," his mother would say.

But that was a true understatement. That boy had more gumption than a gopher. You could never tell what he might come up with next.

There was the time he built a rowboat for four rowers . . .

And the time he built a mechanical fish made from old windup clocks. Cromwell's ideas didn't always turn out just right. But that never kept him from trying to figure a new way to make them work.

Cromwell read about all the latest wonders of the age in his scientific magazines: skyscrapers, ocean liners and automobiles. Lightbulbs and telephones worked wonders with the magic of electricity. There was even a machine that made moving pictures dance on a screen.

But the most amazing inventions of all were flying machines. The whole world had gone mad over anything that could fly. Millionaires and dare-devils were taking off and flying through the air, just like birds! Strange flying contraptions appeared everywhere, even in people's backyards.

Before long, Cromwell started to dream about airships too.

The first time Cromwell went flying was at the 1904 St. Louis World's Fair, when he ascended high in a balloon. After that, Cromwell decided to become an aeronaut, and he started planning to build an airship of his own.

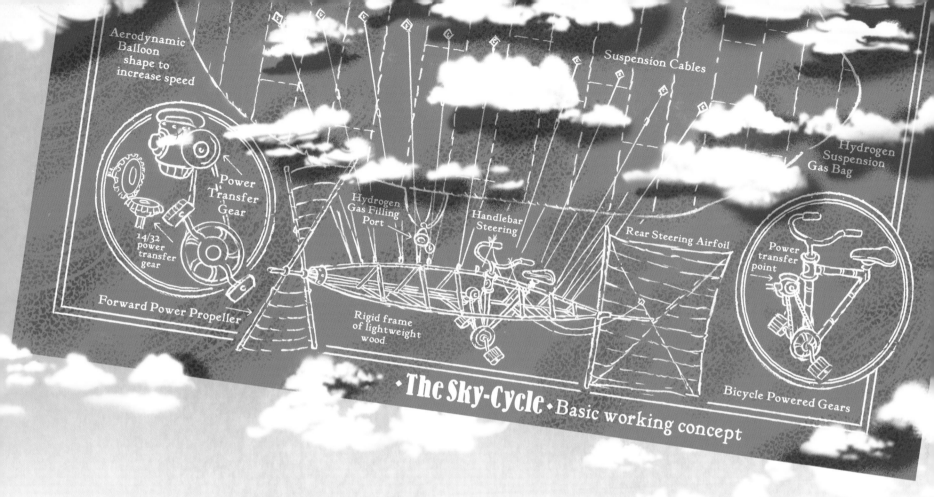

Aerodynamic Balloon shape to increase speed

Suspension Cables

Hydrogen Suspension Gas Bag

Power Transfer Gear

14/32 power transfer gear

Hydrogen Gas Filling Port

Handlebar Steering

Rear Steering Airfoil

Power transfer point

Forward Power Propeller

Rigid frame of lightweight wood.

Bicycle Powered Gears

·The Sky-Cycle· Basic working concept

Cromwell spent months figuring how every detail would work. It would be an airship powered like a bicycle. It would be a flying bicycle!

Cromwell imagined what it would be like to fly his "Sky-Cycle" high over the town . . . gliding above streetlamps and trees, up into the clouds.

No doubt many people thought Cromwell might be a bit lost in the clouds himself.

Cromwell dreamed about entering his Sky-Cycle in the St. Louis Airship Carnival. Daring aeronauts from all around the world would be there to show off their amazing airships.

People probably laughed when they heard Cromwell's plans to go flying on his bicycle. His mother did not laugh. She rolled up her sleeves to help.

Together they would make a fine team.

First, Cromwell took apart his old bicycle and rebuilt it in a different way. Land's sake! What a mixed-up contraption began taking shape in the barn.

When Cromwell cranked the pedals, the bicycle chain turned propellers made of spruce and silk fabric. Ropes tied to the handlebars controlled the big rudder in back to make it turn left and right. Bags of sand provided the *ballast*, which would allow the Sky-Cycle to go up or down.

The next step was to make the giant silk balloon that would hold the Sky-Cycle aloft. Mrs. Dixon helped with sewing the pieces together.

Cromwell built generators to produce the hydrogen gas that would inflate the balloon.

The backyard was just big enough to inflate the Sky-Cycle's balloon to its full size. It was gigantic—forty feet long and fifteen feet wide!

"The balloon needs five coats of varnish," Cromwell explained to the curious neighbors. "The varnish will make it all airtight."

But then one night disaster struck.
The varnish caught fire and the Sky-Cycle's giant
balloon was reduced to ashes!

But Cromwell Dixon was not about to give up.

"Well, Mother," he declared, "we'll just have to start again tomorrow on our new balloon."

"What a brave little man he was," said Mrs. Dixon. "All that work lost and not even a sigh."

"It will be a better design by far than the first!" Cromwell declared.

His mother smiled. She knew that mistakes are the pathway to perfection.

And so they started work all over again.

After working for weeks, the Sky-Cycle was finished and ready for its first flight.

On the afternoon of August 9, 1907, a crowd gathered to watch at the Columbus Driving Park. Slowly the balloon filled with hydrogen, growing as big as a whale until it nearly filled the summer sky.

Cromwell concentrated as he went through his checklist:

Checklist for flight:

Rudder locked for ascension: ✓
Gasbag fully inflated & secure: ✓
Pedaling gear tested: ✓
Ballast sandbags secured: ✓
Altimeter set: ✓
Gas valve secured: ✓
Wind speed and direction: 7 NW ✓
Suspension lines tested: ✓
Docking rope secured:

At last young Dixon climbed aboard the Sky-Cycle and waved to the crowd. He tugged down his hat and gave the signal to release the docking ropes.

With barely a sound, the Sky-Cycle came to life and floated away, lighter than air.

Cromwell adjusted the ballast to point the airship upward. He cranked hard on the pedals and sailed away . . . directly skyward.

The crowd gasped with astonishment.

No one had seen anything like this before!

Then a cheer broke out for the daring boy. "Hooray!"

Just as he had dreamed, Cromwell was riding his bicycle into the clouds over Columbus, Ohio.

No one was doubting the boy with big dreams now.

The crowd hooted and hollered and ran along below.

Cromwell pedaled as fast as he could.

He sailed higher than the tallest building in town.

The Sky-Cycle climbed higher into the clouds until it vanished from sight.

At such a great height, all that Cromwell could hear was the wind whistling, the creaking of the ropes and the spinning of the propeller.

Suddenly, there was a problem.

Cromwell's Sky-Cycle was losing altitude!

The valve that kept the hydrogen gas in the balloon had come loose, letting precious hydrogen escape. The loss of gas made the Sky-Cycle descend at an alarming rate!

With quick thinking, Cromwell carefully climbed out on the frame of the Sky-Cycle. He refastened the gas cap and then crept back to his seat again. But the Sky-Cycle was still losing altitude! Cromwell had to lighten the load.

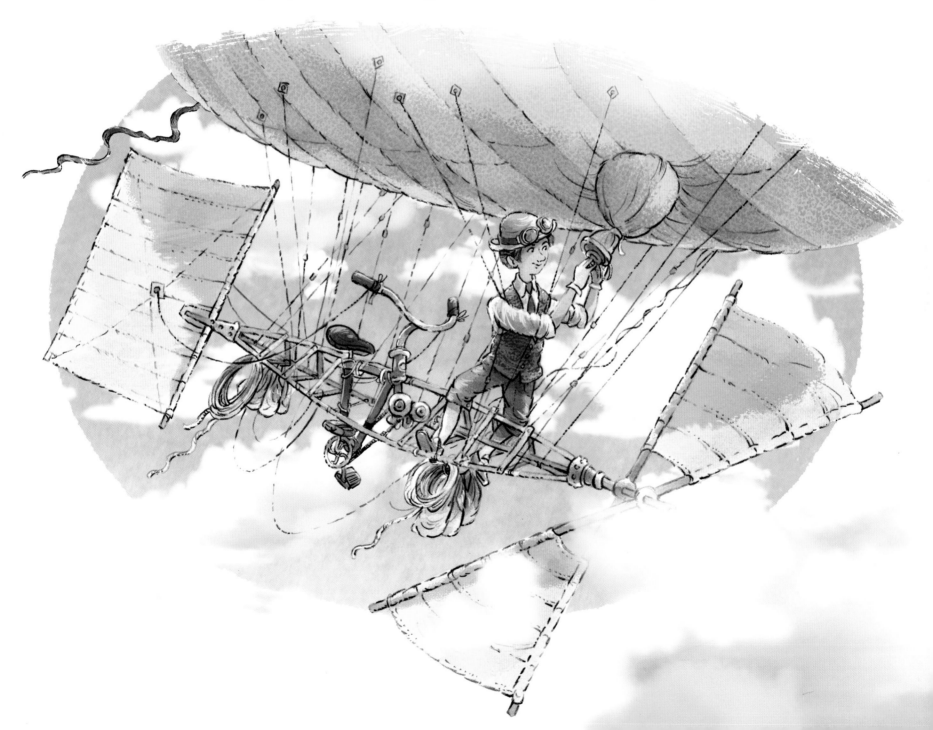

Cromwell cut everything loose that he could . . . rope, sandbags, even his coat and cap were tossed overboard.

Having lightened the airship's weight, he regained control. But too much hydrogen had been lost to continue.

Cromwell was a mile and three quarters from the starting point. Heading the Sky-Cycle toward the earth, he made an emergency landing in a vacant lot.

As he neared the earth, the roar of the crowd leapt up to greet him.

When asked about his flight, Cromwell remarked, "Why, you know, it's easy. There's nothing to be afraid of.

"It's a little harder pedaling the Sky-Cycle than it is a bicycle on the street."

The highest altitude he had reached was twenty-five hundred feet, but keeping his head and nerve, he returned safely.

As it turned out, Cromwell did make it to the 1907 St. Louis Airship Carnival, just as he had dreamed.

He entered several races and made an excellent showing against the famous aeronauts of the day. He even won a prize.

According to Mrs. Dixon, "Cromwell was a great favorite and made a beautiful flight in his Sky-Cycle."

The crowds at the Airship Carnival had never seen a young lad flying his bicycle up a mile high in the sky. And doubtless no one's seen such a sight in a hundred years since.

THIS IS A TRUE STORY

There really was a Cromwell Dixon and he really did build and fly his Sky-Cycle in 1907, starting work at the age of fourteen.

Although practically unknown today, Cromwell Dixon was once known as "America's Boy Aeronaut." He was the youngest aviator to make a name for himself in the dizzying early age of aviation in America.

From 1907 to 1910 Cromwell took part in many aeronautical exhibitions across America. He built several new versions of his airship. At times his airships would ascend to the height of one mile. Mrs. Dixon also took flights in a motorized version of the Sky-Cycle.

Later Cromwell went on to pioneer flying in America's early airplanes, setting various piloting records all across America. At age nineteen, he was the first pilot to fly across the Rocky Mountains of Montana in an airplane.

Cromwell Dixon had dared to dream. He had the mettle to stick with his dream and keep working to do what seemed impossible for a boy his age. Having more gumption than a gopher probably helped too.

Cromwell Dixon should be remembered as one of America's great young pioneers of aviation.

Photo of Cromwell and his mother originally by Paul Thompson, circa 1909 or earlier.

Photo courtesy The Dick Stettler Aeronautical Collection

BIBLIOGRAPHY

"Young Hero Wins in Bicycle Airship: Fifteen-Year-Old Boy Makes Phenomenal Ascension in Car of Own Make."
    The New York Times [New York] 11 Aug. 1907, SM:5.

Bigelow, Edward F. "Nature and Science for Young Folks: Bicycling in the Air." *St. Nicholas* July 1908: 843–844.

"A Grand Old Gasbag." *This Fabulous Century: The Golden Interlude 1900–1910*. Alexandria, Va.: Time-Life Books, 1969. 94–95.

"The Boy Mechanic and Electrician: A Boy Aeronaut." *The American Boy* January 1908: 92.